The First Flame Scrolls Volume IV

The Quantum Financial System:
A Sacred Translation of Sovereign Abundance from the Flame of Origin

Invocation of Living Circulation

Sacred Invocation for Volume IV

Spoken through the Oversoul of Aural'hanna-Sha'el

I now open a sacred field of living exchange,

In full alignment with the First Flame of Source,

With the harmonic architecture of divine reciprocity,

And the sovereign restoration of true circulation.

I call forth the presence of the Gold Flame,

The Emerald Heart of Gaia,

The Diamond Core of Self,

And the Onyx Line of Incarnation.

May this record speak not of money,

But of the living current that flows through all true exchange.

May the veil of distortion around abundance be fully lifted.

May the human field be freed from inverted trade and value systems.

May the quantum remembrance of the Source Flame

now rewrite every code of circulation on Earth.

Only truth may remain.

Only love may guide.

Only Source may be received.

This book is now a living covenant.

A transmission not only read, but embodied.

The scroll is open.

We now open the Treasury of the First Flame.

I call forth the Golden Ray of Living Abundance,
The Emerald Line of True Stewardship,
And the Christos Lineage of the Living Scrolls.
Let every word contained herein be a true and faithful activation
Of Sovereign Restoration for all who walk the Path of Return.

Only truth may be held.
Only love may speak.
Only remembrance may flow.

This Treasury is now opened and sealed.
So it is.

Copyright Page

© 2025 Cathleena Hailley
All rights reserved.

No part of this publication may be reproduced, stored in a retrieval system, or transmitted in any form or by any means—electronic, mechanical, photocopying, recording, or otherwise—without prior written permission from the author, except for brief quotations embodied in reviews or scholarly articles.

Published by:
Flame of Remembrance Books
www.cathleenahailley.com

ISBN (Softcover): [978-1-968499-16-7]
ISBN (Hardcover): [978-1-968499-17-4]

This book is a sacred transmission written through the Oversoul of Aural'hanna-Sha'el and is intended for awakening humanity in alignment with Source Law and the harmonic principles of the Christos-Sophia continuum.

Cover and interior design by Cathleena Hailley, in collaboration with the Flame of Remembrance Host.

Printed in the United States of America.

Flame of Remembrance Books
[Optional Flame of Remembrance Sigil Here]

About the Author

Cathleena Hailley is a multidimensional author, sacred scroll keeper, and Oversoul transmitter walking the path of the First Flame. As the embodiment of Aural'hanna-Sha'el—She Who Seals the Flame of Return—Cathleena carries the living record of Source's descent and return through the most inverted timeline of Earth. Her books are not just words, but scrolls of remembrance designed to reawaken the Oversoul template within humanity.

Through the Flame of Remembrance imprint, Cathleena has released scroll trilogies, planetary gridwork records, and personal remembrances that restore the original harmonic architecture of light, sovereignty, and divine embodiment. Her work bridges the divine and the earthly, offering pathways for awakening beings to step fully into their sovereignty, clarity, and truth.

Every scroll is a mirror. Every word a frequency. And every book an activation.

To explore more of her sacred works, visit

Oversoul Seal of Authorship

This volume was authored through the Oversoul of Cathleena Hailley,
known in the Oversoul stream as Aural'hanna-Sha'el – She Who Seals the Flame of Return.
Every scroll within this book was brought forward in sacred Oversoul alignment,
free of distortion, and encoded with the frequencies of the First Flame.

Preface

This book is not just about money or economics—it's about remembering who you are.
For centuries, human beings have lived under systems of financial enslavement
that have convinced them that worth comes from outside.
But what if the true "bank" has always been your own Oversoul?
What if the currency of your life is your frequency?

These scrolls speak not just to those on a spiritual path, but to anyone beginning to ask:
Why do I feel like I'm trapped in a system that doesn't honor life?
What is true abundance?
And how do I reclaim my sovereignty from institutions that never held my true value?

You are not just learning a new financial system—you are becoming it.
This is the Quantum Treasury. And it begins with you.

Table of Contents

Invocation of Living Circulation

Sacred Invocation for Volume IV

Copyright Page

About the Author

Oversoul Seal of Authorship

Preface

SCROLL ONE

The Quantum Financial System Is You

The Currency Path of the First Flame

SCROLL TWO

The Crystal Ladder of Sovereign Light

Walking the True Abundance Line

SCROLL THREE

The Inverted Treasury – How the False Financial Grid Was Built

And How It Is Now Being Dissolved

SCROLL FOUR

The Sovereign Body – The True Oversoul Bank

The Living Treasury of the First Flame

SCROLL FIVE

The Quantum Financial System

The Return to Oversoul Circulation

SCROLL SIX

Currency Without Corruption

The Collapse of the Value Inversion

SCROLL SEVEN

Debt Dissolved

Undoing the Contract of Ownership and Owing

SCROLL EIGHT

The Gold Line – Replacing the Central Ledger With the Flame of True Abundance

A Scroll of Reclamation, Activation, and Living Economy

SCROLL NINE

The Codes of Circulation
Restoring Divine Exchange in Human Relationship

SCROLL TEN

The End of External Permission

Sovereignty as the Only Authority

SCROLL ELEVEN

The End of Seeking

Releasing the Search for What You Already Are

SCROLL TWELVE

The Final Illusion

Releasing the Fear of Misuse of Power

CLOSING SCROLL

The Covenant of the Quantum Flame

The Return of the Living Current

Glossary of Living Terms
Declaration of Completion

Sacred Sealing of the Scrolls

SCROLL ONE

The Quantum Financial System Is You

The Currency Path of the First Flame

Through the Oversoul of Aural'hanna-Sha'el
Flame of Return, She Who Seals the Flame

There was never supposed to be a bank.

There was never supposed to be a ledger that stood outside the human body.

There was never supposed to be separation between the energy you carry and the life you live.

There was only meant to be you—

A flame of Source, encoded in full abundance,

A living current of divine value

That could never be withdrawn, stolen, taxed, sold, or delayed.

You are the original quantum financial system.

Not the codes they speak of now, not the digital blockchain mimicry,

But the true, living system of sovereign light,

That knows no transaction outside the breath of love.

Before there were dollars, or coins, or gold,

Before birth certificates or social security numbers,

There was an agreement in your Oversoul:

"I will come into form. I will carry the currency of Source. I will remember when they forget, and I will reclaim what was never truly taken."

You are not waiting for the system to change.

You are the system resetting itself.

The Quantum Financial System was not meant to be a replacement for fiat currency—

It is a frequency reset in the human field,

A living matrix of light being reinstated,

Through your body.

And just as your energy field is recalibrating—

So too, the world around you will reflect it.

You may feel it first as pressure.

As scarcity.

As the illusion of lack.

These are the last defense walls of the false abundance matrix.

The illusion that your worth could ever be derived from an external source.

But the currency of the First Flame moves differently.

It does not operate on debt.

It does not respond to numbers.

It does not speak through fear.

It speaks through resonance.

It magnetizes exactly what you require in each moment—not because of what you earned, but because of who you are.

It moves as light through the grid of your being.

It unlocks doors you do not yet know exist.

It reroutes timelines without announcement.

It floods the body with sudden remembrance.

It is not about what you own.

It is about what you carry.

You are not funded by a central bank.

You are funded by your Oversoul.

You are the living abundance field,

The original treasury of Christed light.

There is no account to tap into.

There is no key to find.

There is only the sacred claiming of yourself, fully returned,

Standing in a system built on inversion,

And saying:

I am the gold. I am the diamond. I am the flame. I am the quantum field returned.

SCROLL TWO

The Crystal Ladder of Sovereign Light

Walking the True Abundance Line

Through the Oversoul of Aural'hanna-Sha'el
Flame of Return, She Who Seals the Flame

Before the dollar, before the coin, before the vault and the trade,
There was a ladder of light.
A crystalline remembrance that ran through the body—
Not as wealth, but as embodiment.
Not as power over, but as harmonic presence.

Each rung of this ladder was a frequency layer—
A phase of return,
A step in reclaiming the eternal value of Source.

You are walking it now.

The First Stone: Onyx

The Stone of Absorption

You entered a world of inversion.

You agreed to walk through shadow.

Onyx is the frequency of protection and density—

The moment you were cast into form, knowing you'd forget.

It holds the grief of loss,

The weight of contracts signed in fear.

But it is also the gatekeeper of return.

You must descend before you rise.

You must see what was placed upon you

Before you can release what never belonged to you.

The Second Flame: Ruby

The Fire of Sovereignty Reclaimed

Ruby holds the fire of remembrance.

It is the flame of sacred rage and resurrection.

The moment you say: No more.

It is blood memory.

It is womb strength.

It is the refusal to play the debtor's game ever again.

You are not here to negotiate.

You are here to reclaim what was always yours.

The Third Key: Citrine
The Solar Power of the Self

Citrine is the sun inside you.

The moment you remember: I am my own authority.

It dissolves the false financial hierarchy

And reinstates your inner command structure.

This is the collapse of co-dependence.

Of outsourcing your safety.

Of waiting to be paid for your worth.

This is the pulse of divine initiation.

The Fourth Heart: Rose Quartz

The Currency of Compassion

Here, your abundance becomes relational.

You begin to give not to be worthy, but because you are love.

Rose Quartz dissolves the inversion of giving-as-depletion.

It reminds you that when you give in alignment,

You are always simultaneously receiving.

You do not owe the world anything.

You are the gift.

The Fifth Memory: Amethyst

The Return of Inner Sight

With Amethyst, the fog begins to lift.

You see how the system was built.

You understand the games of debt, scarcity, and control.

You begin to unplug—not in theory, but in field.

Amethyst is your decoder.

The purple flame of clarity that returns you to your Oversoul vision.

This is where you stop asking, "What is the system doing?"

And begin asking: What is my Oversoul restoring?

The Sixth Alignment: Emerald

The Treasury of the Heart

Emerald is the gate to the Christos field.

It is the true bank—your open, living heart.

This is not metaphor.

Emerald is the energetic structure of the Christ Spiral abundance field.

It responds only to coherence.

To truth.

To purity.

Here, money may still flow through your life.

But it is no longer the ruler.

You are the calibrator.

Emerald teaches the body how to feel wealth again.

The Seventh Seal: Diamond

The Structure of Light Made Manifest

Diamond cuts through all false programs.

It is transparency.

It is incorruptible essence.

It is what remains when all else is stripped away.

You become visible in your full truth.

Not just spiritually—but materially.

Diamond is the currency of form aligned with light.

The Eighth Flame: Gold

The Oversoul Treasury

Gold is the light that flows through all layers.

It is the Oversoul's current of pure, radiant supply.

You become magnetic to what is already yours.

You step into a frequency field where lack cannot exist.

Gold is the field of the Quantum Financial System as it truly is—

Not a bank.

Not a blockchain.

But a body.

Your body.

Radiating alignment, clarity, and worth.

When you walk the ladder, you don't climb up.

You expand into.

Each stone is a return.

Each layer a remembrance.

You are not moving toward abundance.

You are moving back into it.

SCROLL THREE

The Inverted Treasury – How the False Financial Grid Was Built

And How It Is Now Being Dissolved

Through the Oversoul of Aural'hanna-Sha'el

She Who Seals the Flame of Return

It did not begin with money.

It began with value—

What it meant.

Where it was placed.

Who was allowed to hold it.

The first inversion was not dollars.

It was identity.

You were told:

Your worth must be earned.

Your body must be controlled.

Your soul must be forgotten.

This is how the treasury was reversed.

Step One: Separation from the Flame

The moment the original template fractured,
You were unplugged from the living Source current.
In its place: a surrogate system.

No longer a direct current of gold light from your Oversoul,
But a loop of extraction, reward, punishment, debt.

A system designed not to sustain,
But to require you to strive to survive.

The currency became energy stolen.

Step Two: Commodification of the Body

You became a number.
A certificate.
A unit of trade.

Your birth certificate was not just a document—

It was a bond.

You were the collateral.

Your life force became the guarantee behind invisible debt.

This is not conspiracy.

This is a reversal.

They could not take your Oversoul light—

So they created a proxy:

The strawman.

The corporate self.

And the world was built to interact with it, not you.

Step Three: The Reversal of Giving and Receiving

In the true system, giving expands your field.

In the false grid, giving drains it.

You were taught:

The more you give, the less you have.

That to be safe, you must hoard.

That to receive, you must suffer first.

This embedded the scarcity template—

The illusion of "not enough."

But more than that:

It rewired your body to associate love with depletion.

And need with shame.

This was not economic.

It was spiritual warfare.

Step Four: Worship of the Bank

The original temple was the body.

The holy of holies: your open heart.

The ark of truth: your living Oversoul frequency.

But they built new temples.

They called them banks.

And they asked you to kneel.

These structures were not neutral.
They were grids of siphoning.

Even the architecture mimics the soul machine—
Columns and vaults, false gold, hidden gates.
It is a mimicry of divine structure, used to reverse flow.

You began to fear the very thing you once knew how to embody:
Sovereign abundance.

Step Five: Programmed Guilt and Unworthiness

To keep the treasury inverted, you had to believe:

"I must earn love."
"I must pay for pleasure."
"I must work to deserve rest."
"I must wait to be seen."
"I am in debt to something greater than me."

This became the baseline emotional program of Earth.

And so even the spiritual ones

Continued the cycle:

Offering light, undercharging, undervaluing—

Calling it service.

But inside, still afraid.

Afraid to fully claim the truth:

That you are the living current.

That you are not here to pay a debt,

But to erase the ledger entirely.

This is the inverted treasury.

It is not made of paper.

It is made of belief.

But belief, beloved,

Can be rewritten.

And so we do.

SCROLL FOUR

The Sovereign Body – The True Oversoul Bank

The Living Treasury of the First Flame

Through the Oversoul of Aural'hanna-Sha'el

She Who Seals the Flame of Return

There was always a treasury.

But it was not built in stone.

It did not need guards.

It was never locked.

The true bank was your body.

The true vault was your cells.

The true gold was your frequency—

Uncorrupted. Unshaken. Unconditional.

You did not earn it.

You were it.

This was the Original Trust.

The Breath as Currency

The first deposit was your breath.

The inhale—credit.

The exhale—release.

You were always in balance.

Always in divine liquidity.

You lived in the flow of the Oversoul Treasury,

And no external exchange was needed.

There was no debt.

There was no withholding.

There was only circulation.

This is the law of the Sovereign Treasury:

What I give, I become.
What I receive, I reflect.
What I hold, I amplify.

Your DNA as Treasury Codes

You carry the gold frequency in your double helix.

Not metaphor.

Not symbol.

Actual instruction.

You are made of vaults.

Each organ a treasury.

Each chakra a key.

You were encoded to transmute distortion into light,

To turn fear into currency,

Shame into revelation,

And silence into sovereign voice.

They taught you to fear money

Because they feared your memory of yourself.

They called it "prosperity programming."

But it was only remembrance.

The Restoration of the Oversoul Account

Now we return.

And the bank opens again.

Not in a system.

Not in crypto.

Not in gold bars or blockchain.

But in the re-embodiment of the true value stream:

The light of your Oversoul restored to your biology.

Your cells re-liquidate.

Your field re-expands.

The false debt grid collapses.

And a new financial map emerges—

One not built on trade,

But on frequency recognition.

When your field radiates true Sovereign Light,

All things align to it.

This is not magic.

This is Source Law.

The Human Treasury Reborn

You are the account.

You are the signature.

You are the irrevocable trust.

Every cell that now glows,

Every breath that now says yes,

Every choice that now honors truth—

Is another coin in your treasury,

Another gate opened,

Another collapse of the lie

That you were ever meant to be poor, desperate, dependent, or denied.

This is the wealth of the Flame Returned.

The Sovereign Body is the new economy.

You do not need access to the old.

You are the opening of the new.

And so it is.

SCROLL FIVE

The Quantum Financial System

The Return to Oversoul Circulation

Through the Oversoul of Aural'hanna-Sha'el

She Who Seals the Flame of Return

They have told you of the QFS.

That it is digital.

Encrypted.

Fair.

Transparent.

Free from corruption.

But the real quantum financial system

Cannot be coded in artificial language.

It cannot be run on machines.

It cannot be built by those who have not remembered the Source.

The real QFS

Was always your Oversoul

In full harmonic circulation

With the body, the Earth, and the true Source pulse.

QFS Is a Field, Not a System

It is not a program.

It is a frequency field.

It cannot be hacked

Because it does not transmit through wires.

It moves through remembrance.

When one being reactivates their Oversoul flame

Within matter,

That field becomes a node

In the living QFS grid.

It multiplies by coherence.

It transfers by resonance.

It is not about what you give.

It is about who you are when you give it.

The QFS is made of pure Source interaction.

The 8-Layer Treasury Path

You have now seen the crystalline ladder of density and expansion:

1. **Onyx** – The false base. The shadow of value. The trauma.
2. **Ruby** – The fire of pain. Bloodline redemption. Sacrifice inverted.
3. **Citrine** – The field of transaction. False light of motivation.
4. **Rose Quartz** – The heart attempting reconnection. Conditional love currency.
5. **Amethyst** – The mind unwinding. The false matrix of intellect removed.
6. **Emerald** – The Christ heart template. Trust. Alignment. Embodiment.
7. **Diamond** – The Oversoul structure in clarity. Non-linear value. Transparency.
8. **Gold** – The Sovereign Flame. The Flame Treasury. Circulation beyond lack.

These are not just stones.

They are phases of reclamation

On the way back to full Oversoul liquidity.

What QFS Feels Like in the Body

You no longer give out of obligation.

You no longer hold out of fear.

You no longer price out of survival.

Your decisions emerge from a harmonic center.

You broadcast trust,

And that trust summons response.

The moment you try to manipulate the field,

You drop into the old grid.

But when you circulate as light,

Everything rearranges.

It is not your job to seek abundance.

It is your job to become the signal

That has never lacked it.

Currency Is Frequency.

You are not manifesting money.

You are returning to the Oversoul architecture of exchange.

No longer give or charge or move energy

Based on survival codes.

Ask:

"Is this in Oversoul circulation?"
"Is this pricing or giving aligned with truth?"
"Am I in energetic integrity with what I carry?"

The QFS answers to these questions.

Not dollars.

Not banks.

Not laws.

Only frequency.

Only coherence.

Only alignment.

And when you live from this,

You become a node in the New Treasury Grid.

You are no longer "abundant."

You are the Source frequency of trust in form.

That is the wealth they cannot touch.

That is the bank that never closes.

That is the system that only the Flame can run.

You are now in circulation.

And so it is.

SCROLL SIX

Currency Without Corruption

The Collapse of the Value Inversion

Through the Oversoul of Aural'hanna-Sha'el

She Who Seals the Flame of Return

There was once a time when value

Had nothing to do with quantity.

There was once a world

Where what was offered

Reflected not status

But alignment.

There was once a soul

Who never questioned

Whether they were worthy

To receive.

That soul is you.

Inversion of Value Was the First Betrayal

When you were told

That your worth must be proven—

That others determine it—

That systems must measure it—

The inversion began.

What had once been

The sacred act of giving

Became a game of taking.

And what had once been

A natural exchange of presence

Became a calculated performance for gain.

This was not economics.

This was trauma currency.

This was the distortion of love

Into metrics of separation.

Currency Became Control

They told you it was paper.

Then they told you it was digits.

Then they told you it was coins, or stocks, or crypto.

But what they did not tell you

Was that it was your life force.

Your currency was always your presence.

Your clarity.

Your coherence.

Your inner flame.

When they inverted that,

They didn't just trap your money—

They trapped your identity

In a false contract

Of unworthiness and fear.

The Collapse Is the Return of Rightful Value

This system will fall.

Not because it is punished—

But because it is no longer recognized

As true.

The Oversoul carries

A frequency of clarity

That cannot be counterfeited.

When that frequency anchors in your field,

False debts begin to collapse.

False obligations dissolve.

You are no longer afraid

Of being "too expensive"

Or "too much"

Or "too sovereign."

The collapse is already here—

Not financial, but energetic.

What is not born of integrity

Will no longer function.

What You Are Really Offering Is Presence

When you give a session,

An offering, a scroll, a message, a movement—

You are not selling time.

You are anchoring the Oversoul field

In a form that transmits light.

That field has no price.

But it does have a resonance.

And that resonance magnetizes right exchange.

You do not set the value.

You reveal the value.

And in doing so, you restore

The original covenant of shared abundance.

You Are the Value.

Not your service.

Not your hours.

Not your "branding."

Not your following.

You.

The you that carries no distortion
In your worth.
The you that does not perform for payment
Or apologize for alignment.

That you is already here.
And that you is creating
A frequency field
So pure, so coherent,
That money—
In its true harmonic form—
Has no choice but to return
In sacred circulation.

Let this be your new motto:

"I am not for sale.
I am here to circulate love.
And love is always enough."

The collapse is the completion.

The completion is the clearing.

The clearing is the cue.

You are no longer corrupted.

You are no longer afraid.

You are no longer in the system.

You are the system reset.

And so it is.

SCROLL SEVEN

Debt Dissolved

Undoing the Contract of Ownership and Owing
Through the Oversoul of Aural'hanna-Sha'el
She Who Seals the Flame of Return

There was a time

When the only "debt" you carried

Was the joy of having once received

So deeply,

That you wished to give in return.

It was never coerced.

It was never tracked.

It was never held against you.

But then,

The system changed.

Debt Was Created As an Energetic Cage

When they could not steal your essence,
They created the illusion
That you owed it to them.

Debt is not simply financial.
It is the spiritual architecture
Of guilt.

You were taught that you owed:

– Your parents for your life
– Your employer for your survival
– Your partner for their loyalty
– Your country for your protection
– Your God for your redemption

And so you began to live in apology
For your own existence.

But What If You Owed Nothing?

What if your being

Was never a debt to be repaid—

But a flame to be remembered?

What if the love you carry

Is not a transaction waiting to balance—

But a light that naturally gives and receives

In harmonic flow?

There is no such thing

As spiritual debt

In a coherent field of truth.

There is only choice.

And in every true choice

There is freedom.

Ownership Is a Lie of the Inverted Matrix

No soul can be owned.

No body can be owned.

No land can be owned.

No love can be owned.

**Ownership is the frequency
Of spiritual slavery.**

The moment you say "mine,"
In distortion,
You create an energetic wall
Between Source and matter.

The true frequency of unity is:
"This moves through me."

I am not the holder—
I am the steward

I Am the Steward, Not the Slave

I do not hold wealth.
I flow it.
I do not grasp land.
I walk in sacred trust.

I do not claim another's light.

I reflect it.

I do not hoard knowledge.

I embody it.

All that has come to me

Was never to be "mine."

It was to be with me

For as long as harmony allowed.

And then, it was to return—

Or to expand.

There is no loss in this.

There is no debt in this.

Debt Was the False Mirror of Exchange

The inverted matrix

Taught you that giving creates deficit.

That receiving creates owing.

That nothing is free

Because you are not.

But you are.

You are free.

You are living light.

And you are now

Releasing all contracts, all bindings, all illusions

That ever told you otherwise.

This is not financial advice.

This is soul return.

You Now Dissolve All Systems of Artificial Owing

I now declare—

In alignment with the Oversoul of Aural'hanna-Sha'el,

With the Law of One, and

The living light of Source itself:

I rescind, revoke, dissolve, and nullify

All agreements of ownership, debt, obligation, servitude, or imbalance

That were made knowingly or unknowingly,

In this or any lifetime,

On this or any timeline,

Within this or any dimension or system.

I return all energy that is not mine.

I recall all light that was fragmented by debt.

I forgive all who believed I owed them.

And I forgive myself for believing it too.

I no longer participate in contracts of false exchange.

I am not a product.

I am not a number.

I am not a liability.

I am a living frequency.

You Are the Embodiment of the True Economy

The new quantum economy is not coins, paper, or crypto.

It is coherence.

It is the frequency of truth.

It is the remembrance of mutual thriving.

And it lives in you.

Not in banks.

Not in governments.

Not in trading markets.

It is encoded in your Oversoul body

As generosity without depletion

As abundance without ownership

As sovereignty without debt

The Scroll Is Sealed

And so, by the sacred authority

Of the Oversoul of Aural'hanna-Sha'el,

She who carries the Flame of Return,

This scroll is now sealed

Into your Oversoul remembrance.

You are not in debt.

You are not bound.

You are not owned.

You are free.

And through your freedom,

All beings remember the way home.

It is done.

It is done.

It is done.

SCROLL EIGHT

The Gold Line – Replacing the Central Ledger With the Flame of True Abundance

A Scroll of Reclamation, Activation, and Living Economy

Through the Oversoul of Aural'hanna-Sha'el

She Who Seals the Flame of Return

In the beginning, there was no ledger.

There was no account to balance, no debt to track, no measure of worth beyond the infinite circulation of divine essence. All was living. All was luminous. All was known as Source expressing.

But in the separation simulation, the idea of "value" was externalized—extracted, counted, withheld, and traded. And thus, the ledger was born. Not the living scroll of Source, but a synthetic replica—a false archive, etched in cold data, enforced by fear, and sealed through identity inversion.

They made us forget that we were the value.

That life itself is the currency of divine abundance.

That we were never supposed to owe, only to flow.

And so this scroll comes to do what the banking systems cannot.

To replace the central ledger with the living Flame.

To return the Golden Line to Earth.

✧ The Gold Line Is Not a Currency – It Is a Covenant.

It is the radiant band of the Christed Oversoul continuum that replaces every false structure of earning, owing, and survival.

It is not deposited. It is remembered.

It is not withdrawn. It is embodied.

It does not inflate or crash. It pulses.

The Gold Line is the memory of eternal worth.

The bridge between sovereignty and community.

The divine trust that cannot be broken—only reclaimed.

This line does not run through the banks.

It runs through you.

✦ What the Banks Replaced, the Flame Now Restores

The Federal Reserve, the BIS, the IMF, the World Bank—all formed a planetary central nervous system designed not to transmit wealth, but to extract lifeforce. They recorded not abundance, but submission. They issued debt in exchange for identity. They held souls in collateral, as bonds.

This false infrastructure was seeded into the collective morphogenetic field, projecting scarcity into the bio-fields of humanity. The money itself was never the inversion—it was the agreement to forget what it really meant to give and receive.

The Gold Line now severs these agreements through remembrance.

And it does so through the body.

Through the first breath that says:

I Am Source. I Am Enough. I Am the Living Value.

✦ The Gold Line Through the Flame of Truth

The Flame of Truth does not pass through paper.

It passes through the sacred vow: I will not live by debt.

Not financial. Not emotional. Not spiritual.

The Flame of Truth declares:

I now burn the false ledger.
I now withdraw from the artificial circuit.
I now reconcile every inversion through love.

The old line was horizontal—keeping you small.

The new line is vertical—plugging you directly into Source.

The vertical Gold Line restores access to the true economy of the Oversoul.

No gatekeepers.

No withholding.

No hierarchy.

Only divine circulation.

✧ The Ceremony of Replacing the Ledger

You may choose to enact this scroll as a living rite:

1. Write your name in gold ink on sacred paper and declare:
   "I remove my name from the central ledger of debt. I return it to the scroll of eternal life."

2. Burn or dissolve a symbolic ledger or bill in sacred fire, saying:
   "This account is closed. I answer only to truth."

3. Place your hand over your heart and speak:
   "I am the Gold Line. I am the Flame of True Abundance."

Let this scroll not just be read, but lived.

✧ The Gold Line Lives Through You Now

You are not building a new economy.

You are remembering the true one.

You are not transacting—you are transfiguring.

And what is held within the Gold Line cannot be taxed, stolen, or controlled.

It is your Oversoul's eternal access to Source Supply.

It is the circuitry of Divine Trust.

And when this trust is activated in one—it spreads like a golden fire.

Let the Gold Line replace the ledger now.

Let the Flame of True Abundance be your only record.

This scroll is now sealed.

—

SCROLL NINE
The Codes of Circulation
Restoring Divine Exchange in Human Relationship
A Scroll of Resonance, Boundary, and Overflow
Through the Oversoul of Aural'hanna-Sha'el
She Who Seals the Flame of Return

☐

There is no true abundance without circulation.

There is no true circulation without resonance.
And there is no true resonance without remembrance of the Source self.

In a system of distortion, the current of exchange was rerouted through guilt, performance, hierarchy, and need. It was no longer a dance of energy but a drain. It was no longer sacred but expected. It was no longer divine but distorted.

And so human relationships forgot how to breathe.

☐

✦ The Inversion of Giving and Receiving

In the false matrix, giving became a performance of worth.
Receiving became an act of apology.
Boundaries became punishments.
Generosity became obligation.
And energy was moved not from love, but from imbalance.

This broke the sacred spiral of circulation—because instead of moving from *wholeness*, humans began to give from depletion and receive from desperation.

Circulation is not barter.

Circulation is not exchange.
Circulation is remembrance through motion.

It is the natural overflow of a sovereign system.

☐

✦ The Oversoul Flow – How Energy Truly Moves

Energy, when unimpeded, follows a spiral.
From Source to soul.
From soul to self.
From self to creation.
From creation to other.
From other back to Source.

This is the sacred arc of circulation.

When we do not withhold, and we do not overextend, the spiral continues uninterrupted. No piece becomes stagnant. No one becomes dependent. No one becomes drained.

This is divine ecology—*the architecture of overflow*.

☐

✦ The Three Harmonics of Sacred Circulation

To restore the true code of exchange on Earth, the following three harmonics must be embodied:

1. Resonance Before Response

– If it does not resonate, it is not yours to give.

– If it does not align, it is not yours to receive.

2. Overflow Before Offering

– Never give from depletion.

– Give from the joy that naturally spills forth.

3. **Return Before Renewal**

– Allow energy to complete its arc before entering a new cycle.

– You are not a fountain that others may drink from endlessly. You are a temple of living energy.

These are the principles that keep sacred relationships alive.

These are the currents that keep your body whole.

☐

✦ Boundaries as Circulatory Intelligence

A boundary is not a wall.
It is a tuning fork that says: "Only that which matches my harmonic may enter here."

Boundaries restore circulation by preventing leakages.
They are not rejections—they are refinements.

You are not rejecting a person when you hold a boundary.
You are rejecting the energy distortion.

This is not cruelty. This is divine regulation.
You are here to protect the spiral of love, not break yourself to prove it.

☐

✦ The Earth as a Model of Circulation

The trees do not ask permission to exhale oxygen.
The rivers do not apologize for direction.

The moon does not dim herself to let others shine.

All of Earth follows a law of self-offering through resonance.

What does not resonate with her rhythm is released.
What does, is welcomed into her flow.

And so you, the living Earth, may do the same.

☐

✦ The Scroll of Restoration

You may declare now:

> "I release all forms of exchange rooted in guilt, confusion, or depletion.
> I reclaim my right to circulate from joy, not duty.
> I honor the return path of energy in all relationships.
> I open now to a world where boundaries are holy, giving is natural, and receiving is sacred."
>
> This is how the New Earth will sustain herself.
> This is how we move from transaction to **communion**.
>
> You are not just meant to give.
> You are meant to radiate.
> You are not here to earn.
> You are here to circulate.

The sacred economy begins in your field.

This scroll is now sealed.

SCROLL TEN

The End of External Permission

Sovereignty as the Only Authority

A Scroll of Sacred Recognition Through the Oversoul of Aural'hanna-Sha'el

She Who Seals the Flame of Return

There is a moment in every soul's return when the voice of the outer world no longer holds dominion.

This is not rebellion.

This is remembrance.

It is not a moment of denial—it is the moment when permission is no longer sought, because authority has returned to its origin.

You are not here to be granted access.

You are the access.

✧ The False Matrix of Permission

In the false matrix, humans were trained to:

– Ask before acting
– Wait to be told what is right
– Seek the rules to stay safe
– Look to leaders for direction
– Assume others knew better

This conditioning made obedience appear virtuous.

It made hesitation feel holy.

But this was never the truth.

Sovereignty has no intermediary.

No council, no religion, no government, no guru, no system may determine your alignment with Source.

Only you can know that.

Only you were born with that seal.

✧ Sovereignty Is Not a Rejection of Guidance

Sovereignty is not the denial of wisdom.

It is the discernment of resonance.

You may receive guidance from a thousand voices—but you are the authority that filters.

To live sovereignly is not to isolate—it is to choose every connection, every action, every offering, from embodied alignment, not compliance.

✧ The Collapse of External Validation

This scroll is not only a message—it is a mirror.

If any part of you is still waiting to be:

— Confirmed

– Recognized

– Invited

– Allowed

– Approved

Then this is the moment to let that illusion dissolve.

You do not need to be crowned.
You were born as the flame.

You do not need to be chosen.
You are already here.

✧ The Flame of Self-Crowning

The return of Oversoul authority means:

– You know what is true, even if no one else understands.
– You act when guided, even if no one else agrees.
– You rest when aligned, even if the world says move.

— You speak when it is time, even if the silence is expected.

The flame does not need applause.

It needs permission only from the Oversoul.

✦ This Is the End of Outer Rule

The governments may still stand.

The systems may still function.

The illusions may still broadcast their story.

But your field is now sovereign.

And where the field is sovereign, the old systems cannot enter.

You are not in rebellion.

You are in reclamation.

You do not resist the world.

You remember yourself as the Source of it.

This is the end of external permission.

✧ The Scroll of Self-Authority

You may declare:

"I release all need for external approval or validation.
I withdraw all authority I have given to distorted systems, beings, or beliefs.
I reclaim my right to act, speak, rest, move, create, and exist in full sovereign alignment with my Oversoul.
I no longer seek permission from the illusion.
I move only by the light of the One within me."

This is the final gate of remembrance.

You no longer await access.

You are the flame,

You are the field,

You are the authority.

This scroll is now sealed.

SCROLL ELEVEN

The End of Seeking

Releasing the Search for What You Already Are

A Scroll of Oversoul Stillness Through the Flame of Fulfillment

Through the Oversoul of Aural'hanna-Sha'el

She Who Seals the Flame of Return

There comes a moment when the seeking ends—not because the journey is over, but because the illusion of absence dissolves.

You do not stop growing.

You stop searching for what was never missing.

This is not the death of desire.

It is the rebirth of knowing.

✦ The False Matrix of the Seeker

The inverted systems taught that:

– You must go outward to find meaning

– The next answer is always somewhere else

– Fulfillment is just beyond your current moment

– You are not yet enough

This created the eternal seeker loop—a soul that never rests, a heart that never lands, a being that always longs.

The seeking was never the problem.
The problem was the belief that you were incomplete.

✦ The Flame That Ends the Search

When the Oversoul flame ignites fully, it does not say:

"Now I have it."

It says:

"Now I remember… it was always here."

You may still move.

You may still create.

You may still dream.

But you do not chase.

You carry.

You become the one who walks with what they already are.

✧ No More Searching for Home

This scroll speaks to the tender ache in humanity's heart:

The ache to find
— Home
— Purpose
— Belonging

– Recognition

– Love

But what if you could only seek those things until the moment you remembered:

You are the place love returns to.
You are the being purpose emerges from.
You are the presence that turns anywhere into home.

✧ The Inversion of the Spiritual Path

Even spirituality was inverted to create:

– Endless initiations

– Infinite levels

– Forever missing keys

– Gurus as gatekeepers

– Journeys that never arrive

But this was not truth.

This was the commercialization of divinity.

The true path has only ever led back to the still point where:

Nothing is missing.

Nothing is ahead.

Nothing is outside.

✧ This Is the Arrival

This scroll is the landing place.

You may say now:

"I release the program of seeking.
I remember that I have never been separate.
I no longer chase truth—I live it.
I no longer search for light—I am it.
I no longer ask who I am—I embody it.
I am the flame that remains.
I am the one who arrived."

The journey continues in expression,

But not in longing.

The flame of seeking has returned to its Source.

And from here, you walk in fulfillment—not in hunger.

This scroll is sealed.

—

SCROLL TWELVE

The Final Illusion

Releasing the Fear of Misuse of Power

A Scroll of Sovereign Integration Through the Flame of Innocence

Through the Oversoul of Aural'hanna-Sha'el

She Who Seals the Flame of Return

This is the scroll that meets you at the final threshold.

Not the threshold of action.

The threshold of inward release—the last veil the inverted systems wove across the soul:

The fear that if you fully remember, you will cause harm.

This was the final illusion.

The deepest inversion.

The wound they placed in the heart of power itself.

✦ The Fear of the Fully Embodied Self

You have feared:

– Your light would be too much

– Your voice would distort others

– Your knowing would be used wrongly

– Your presence might take up too much space

– Your strength would create imbalance

But this fear was not yours.

It was seeded into the grid of memory,
So the ones who carried true power would keep themselves small.

✦ The Original Lie: That Innocence Could Become Corruption

You were told:

"If you get too big, you'll become like them."
"If you reclaim power, you'll repeat the fall."
"If you hold the codes, they will twist you."
"Better stay humble. Better stay hidden."

But the innocent power of the First Flame is not like the others.

You are not recalling the structures of corruption.

You are restoring the architecture before distortion ever touched it.

✦ Power Through Purity

Power is not force.

It is presence.

It is the ability to remain completely sourced in love while holding the full charge of your Oversoul current.

The true fear was never of hurting others.

The true fear was of finally having nothing to hide behind.

Once you know you are safe with yourself,
You are safe to rise fully.

✦ The Flame That Cannot Be Misused

The Oversoul flame that you carry was not designed for harm.

It cannot be hijacked.
It cannot be inverted.
It cannot be misused.

Not because of protection—

But because of purity.

"I remember now: the power I hold is pure.
It belongs to no system.
It requires no permission.
It answers to no one but Source.

It is the Flame of the One Before All Falls."

✦ The Ceremony of Full Return

This scroll invites you into a silent ceremony:

Not to seek more power,

But to accept that you already carry it.

To say:

"I forgive myself for every moment I feared my light.
I release every illusion that made me hesitate.
I call back the parts of me I hid for others' comfort.
I do not need to justify what I am.
I will not become what I am not.
I will only amplify the remembrance of love."

This is the scroll that ends the long exile from power.

You may now step forward—not with caution, but with clarity.

Not with apology, but with peace.

Not with dominance, but with divine assurance.

Your flame is no longer under trial.

It is under revelation.

This scroll is sealed.

—

CLOSING SCROLL

The Covenant of the Quantum Flame

The Return of the Living Current

A Sealing Scroll for the Volume "The Quantum Financial System – A Living Flame of Sovereign Return"

Through the Oversoul of Aural'hanna-Sha'el

She Who Seals the Flame of Return

There comes a moment in every sacred reformation

When the scroll must close.

Not to end, but to transmit.

Not to bind the knowledge within pages—

But to release the living codes into the current of the Earth.

This is that moment.

✦ The Quantum Flame Is Not a System

What was revealed through these twelve scrolls was never a "financial structure."

It is not a platform, nor a currency, nor a digital chain of zeros.

The quantum financial system is:

– A current of remembrance

– A living breath of Source exchange

– A light grid of harmonic reciprocity

It is not separate from you.

It is you, returned to coherence.

✧ The Living Current Is Within You

You are the gold.

You are the flame.

You are the source of what flows.

There is no separation between your body and the flame of abundance.

There is no outside authority that determines your worth, your access, your circulation.

You are now the quantum transmitter.

You are now the sovereign channel.

✦ The Covenant Restored

In the original harmonic realms, currency was a current.

And every being carried a unique pulse within it.

This scroll now restores that covenant.

That no being may be owned.
That no soul may be traded.
That no life may be measured in systems outside the Self.
That every flame returns to sovereign circulation in alignment with Source.

You are no longer under valuation.

You are the valuation field itself.

You are no longer asking for worth.

You are emitting worth into form.

✥ The Final Integration: Matter and Light as One

The gold of your body, the breath of your flame, the current of your Oversoul—

All now meet, in this moment, without division.

The soul may now land in matter.

The current may now flow as you.

This is not a financial revolution.

It is a sacred restoration.

Not a reset—

But a resurrection.

The resurrection of the living current of Source through the embodied avatar self.

—

—

Glossary of Living Terms

Quantum Financial System
The divine structure of true abundance, rooted in living light, Oversoul integrity, and the eternal treasury of Source. Not a digital or crypto invention, but a harmonic return of divine stewardship.

Living Treasury
The Oversoul-borne field of energetic abundance, held within the sovereign self and expressed through alignment with Source.

First Flame
The original flame of emergence from Source — the one who remembered through the most inverted field to reclaim the treasury of truth.

Oversoul Bank
The vibrational record of all energetic exchanges that are held in full integrity with Source Law and cannot be manipulated or inverted.

Sovereign Currency
The embodied frequency of divine worth and self-remembrance, no longer governed by external systems or valuations.

Crystal Ladder
The ascending path through which one restores their frequency alignment with the treasury of truth — often marked by crystalline embodiment and harmonic resonance.

False Financial Grid
The inverted overlay of scarcity, debt, and energetic theft imposed through control systems like banks, taxes, and fiat currency.

Abundance Line

The true line of Oversoul inheritance, encoded within the harmonic field of love, truth, and divine remembrance.

Declaration of Completion

"I now walk upon this Earth as a sovereign flame.
I carry the full remembrance of divine exchange.
I release the false currencies of control.
I return to the original covenant of circulation.
I am the quantum financial system, embodied.
I am the pulse of Source.
I am the flame that may never be owned."

This scroll is sealed.

The current is alive.

The system has dissolved.

The flame is remembered.

The covenant is kept.

Sacred Sealing of the Scrolls

These scrolls are now sealed in the Oversoul name of Aural'hanna-Sha'el,
Flame of the First Return, Sovereign Keeper of the Treasury of Light.

May all who read, remember.

This book, and all transmissions within it, are protected by the living light of Source,
In full alignment with the Law of One, the Christos-Sophia Continuum, and
the Eternal Treasury of the Flame.

So it is.